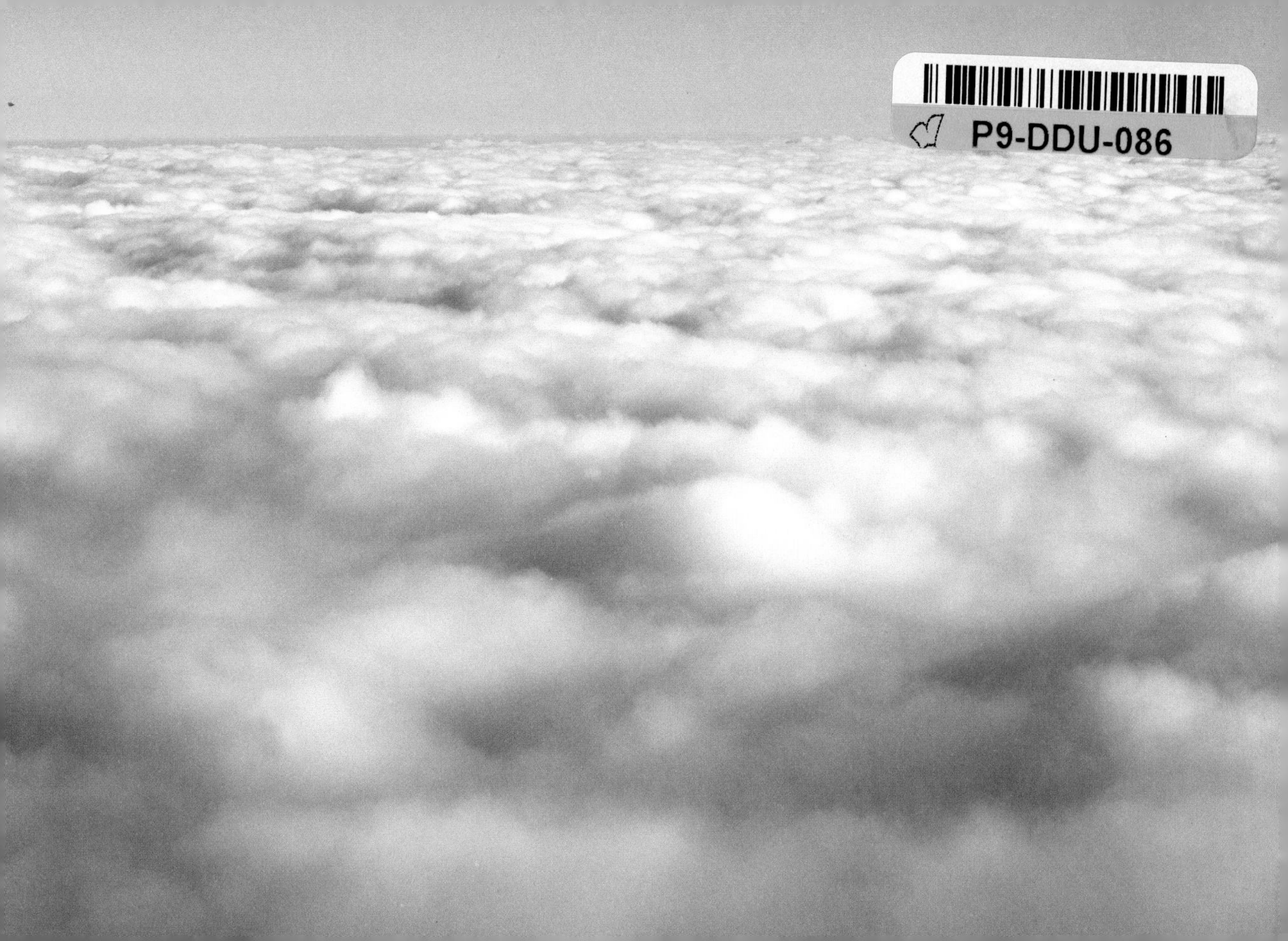

THE POWER OF JOY
Knowing God through the Psalms

CRYSTAL CATHEDRAL

FRONT COVER *Sunflowers, Gunnedah, New South Wales, Australia*
BACK COVER *Rainbow, Victoria Falls, Zimbabwe*
ENDPAPERS *Blue Ridge Parkway, North Carolina, USA*
TITLE PAGE *Chilli Beach, Queensland, Australia*
THIS PAGE *Fruit Bat Falls, Queensland, Australia*
NEXT PAGE *Pipeline, North Shore, Oahu, Hawaii, USA*

INTRODUCTION
by Robert H. Schuller

What is the secret of real joy? Christians know the answer. Real joy is love—the kind that bubbles up from deep within your heart and soul. It tears you away from your own interests to care for someone else. It bears another's burdens. It shares another's journey in joyful moments, tearful moments, and prayerful moments. Love activated is JOY liberated!

Joy cannot be contained. It must break out in praise through songs of thanksgiving. This is what we see all through the psalms. Even when going through the darkest of nights, the psalmist concludes: "…Weeping may endure for a night, but joy comes in the morning" (Psalm 30:5).

No one has more brilliantly captured the essence of joy in photographic form than our great friend Ken Duncan. I pray that as you read the words of the psalms that accompany Ken's Panographs God will put a song in your heart and bring a smile to your face.

DR. ROBERT H. SCHULLER, FOUNDING PASTOR
CRYSTAL CATHEDRAL, HOUR OF POWER

3

PSALM 66:1

Shout for joy to God,
all the earth!

PSALM 95:1

*Come, let us sing
for joy to the LORD;
let us shout aloud
to the Rock
of our salvation.*

My lips will shout for joy
when I sing praise to you—
I, whom you have redeemed.

PREVIOUS PAGE
Bridal Veil Falls, Yosemite Valley,
California, USA

THIS PAGE
Liffey Falls, Tasmania, Australia

Shout for joy to the LORD,
all the earth,
burst into jubilant song with music;
With trumpets and the blast
of the ram's horn—
shout for joy before the LORD,
the King.
Let the rivers clap their hands,
let the mountains sing together for joy.

THIS PAGE
Upper Tahquamenon Falls, Michigan, USA

Let the fields be jubilant,
and everything in them;
let all the trees of the forest
sing for joy.

THIS PAGE
Sunrise over the Sea of Galilee,
Mount of Beatitudes, Israel

For you make me glad
by your deeds, LORD;
I sing for joy
at what your hands have done.

THIS PAGE
Hopetoun Falls, Victoria, Australia

NEXT PAGE
Flamingoes, Al Reem Island,
Abu Dhabi, UAE

PSALM 65:8,13

*The whole earth is filled
with awe at your wonders;
where morning dawns,
where evening fades,
you call forth songs of joy.
The meadows are covered
with flocks and the valleys
are mantled with grain;
they shout for joy and sing.*

Sing joyfully to the LORD,
you righteous;
it is fitting for the upright
to praise him.

THIS PAGE
Giraffes, Sir Bani Yas Island,
Abu Dhabi, UAE

May the nations be glad
and sing for joy,
for you rule the peoples with equity
and guide the nations of the earth.

THIS PAGE
Elephants, Mt. Kilimanjaro, Tanzania

*Our mouths were filled
with laughter,
our tongues with songs of joy.
Then it was said
among the nations,
"The LORD has done
great things for them."
The LORD has done
great things for us,
and we are filled with joy.*

THIS PAGE
Havasu Falls, Arizona, USA

Sing to him a new song;
play skillfully,
and shout for joy.

THIS PAGE
Terrigal sunrise,
New South Wales, Australia

I will go to the altar of God,
to God, my joy and my delight.
I will praise you with the lyre,
O God, my God.

THIS PAGE
Padre Bay, Lake Powell,
Utah, USA

*Satisfy us in the morning
with your unfailing love,
that we may sing for joy
and be glad all our days.*

THIS PAGE
*The Twelve Apostles,
Victoria, Australia*

NEXT PAGE
*Dorrigo National Park,
New South Wales, Australia*

PSALM 94:19

When anxiety was great within me,
your consolation brought me joy.

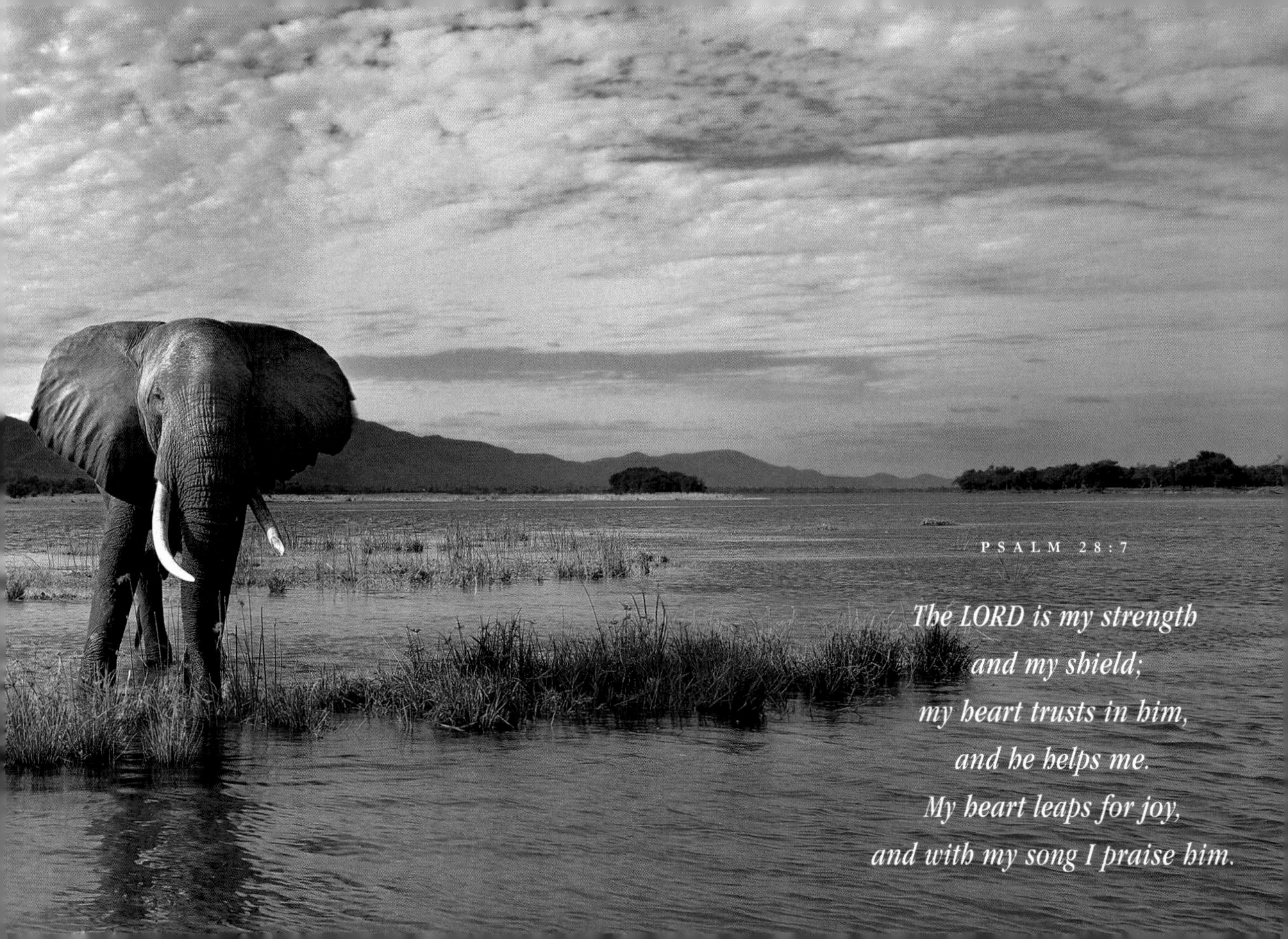

PSALM 28:7

The LORD is my strength
and my shield;
my heart trusts in him,
and he helps me.
My heart leaps for joy,
and with my song I praise him.

Your statutes
are my heritage forever;
they are the joy of my heart.

PREVIOUS PAGE
Elephant, Mana Pools,
Zambezi River, Zimbabwe

THIS PAGE
Sunrise, Cape Byron Lighthouse,
Byron Bay, New South Wales, Australia

Restore to me the joy
of your salvation
and grant me a willing spirit,
to sustain me.

THIS PAGE
Moss Glen Falls, Vermont, USA

The precepts of the LORD are right,
giving joy to the heart.
The commands of the LORD
are radiant,
giving light to the eyes.

THIS PAGE
Long Boat Key, The Keys, Florida, USA

Those who sow with tears
will reap with songs of joy.
Those who go out weeping,
carrying seed to sow,
will return with songs of joy,
carrying sheaves with them.

Sing for joy to God
our strength;
shout aloud
to the God of Jacob!

PREVIOUS PAGE
Wheat Fields, Blaine, Idaho, USA

THIS PAGE
Fijian Islands, Fiji

You make known to me
the path of life;
you will fill me
with joy in your presence,
with eternal pleasures
at your right hand.

THIS PAGE
Sunset, Breakwater Lighthouse,
Cape Henlopen State Park, Delaware, USA

*You turned my wailing
into dancing;
you removed my sackcloth
and clothed me with joy.*

THIS PAGE
Crested Butte, Colorado, USA

Bring joy to your servant, Lord,
for I put my trust in you.

THIS PAGE
Dauphin Island, Alabama, USA

Then my head will be exalted
above the enemies who surround me;
at his tabernacle I will sacrifice
with shouts of joy;
I will sing and make music
to the LORD.

THIS PAGE
Langford Reef, Whitsundays,
Queensland, Australia

PSALM 68:3

But may the righteous
be glad and rejoice before God;
may they be happy and joyful.

But let all who take refuge
in you be glad;
let them ever sing for joy.
Spread your protection over them,
that those who love your name
may rejoice in you.

PREVIOUS PAGE
Chimney Rock, Nebraska, USA

THIS PAGE
Black Mountain Overlook,
Blue Ridge Parkway, North Carolina, USA

*Light shines on the righteous
and joy on the upright in heart.*

THIS PAGE
*Field of Tulips, Skagit Valley,
Washington, USA*

Shout for joy to the LORD,
all the earth.
Worship the LORD with gladness;
come before him with joyful songs.

Let them sacrifice
thank offerings
and tell of his works
with songs of joy.

THIS PAGE
Monongabela National Forest,
West Virginia, USA

Clap your hands,
all you nations;
shout to God
with cries of joy.
God has ascended
amid shouts of joy,
the LORD amid
the sounding of trumpets.

THIS PAGE
American Falls, Niagara Falls,
New York, USA

Kapuaiwa Coconut Grove, Molokai, Hawaii, USA

THE POWER OF JOY
Knowing God through the Psalms
First published 2009
for *Hour of Power*
by Panographs Publishing Pty Ltd
ABN 21 050 235 606
PO Box 3015 Wamberal NSW 2260
Australia
Telephone +61 2 4367 6777
Email: panos@kenduncan.com

Scripture quotations used in this book are
from *Today's New International Version*®
Copyright ©2001, 2005 by International
Bible Society. Used by permission. All rights
reserved.

Photography by Ken Duncan
©2009 Divine Guidance P/L
Designed by Good Catch Design
Reprographics by CFL Print Studio

Printed and bound by Everbest Printing
Co Ltd., China
ISBN 9780 9805278 03

To view the range of Ken Duncan's
panoramic Limited Edition Prints visit the
Ken Duncan Gallery online:
www.kenduncan.com
To visit *Hour of Power* website:
www.hourofpower.org